Cold Start Wealth

Cold Start Wealth

Matthew Petchinsky

1

Cold Start Wealth: Building Financial Power from a Standing Still Point

By: Matthew Petchinsky

Disclaimer

This book, *Cold Start Wealth: Building Financial Power from a Standing Still Point*, is provided for **informational and educational purposes only**. It is not intended to be, and should not be interpreted as, **financial, investment, tax, legal, accounting, or professional advice** of any kind.

The content within this book is based on general principles, conceptual frameworks, and hypothetical examples intended to explore financial thinking, behavioral patterns, and strategic mindset development. **All examples, scenarios, figures, and case studies presented are illustrative and hypothetical**, and do not represent real individuals, businesses, portfolios, or financial outcomes.

Financial circumstances vary widely between individuals. What may be effective for one person may not be appropriate or effective for another. Readers are strongly encouraged to **consult with qualified professionals**, such as licensed financial advisors, certified public accountants, tax professionals, attorneys, or other relevant experts, before making any financial, investment, tax, or legal decisions.

The author does not guarantee any specific financial results, income levels, wealth accumulation, or outcomes from the application of the ideas, concepts, strategies, or frameworks discussed in this book. **Past performance, hypothetical outcomes, or conceptual models do not guarantee future results.**

By reading this book, the reader acknowledges that **all financial decisions involve risk**, including the potential loss of money, time, or opportunity. The reader assumes full responsibility for their own actions, decisions, and results. The author expressly **disclaims any and all liability** for losses, damages, or adverse outcomes—financial or otherwise—that may arise directly or indirectly from the use, application, or interpretation of the information contained in this book.

This book does not promote get-rich-quick schemes, guaranteed income claims, or unrealistic financial promises. It is intended to support **independent thinking, personal responsibility, and informed decision-making**.

Nothing in this book should be construed as an endorsement of any specific investment, financial product, business structure, or strategy. Any references to tools, methods, or approaches are provided solely for conceptual discussion.

By engaging with this material, the reader agrees that the author and publisher are **not acting as fiduciaries**, advisors, or agents, and that the relationship between the reader and the author is purely that of an informational content provider and consumer.

Introduction

Why January Is Not About Motivation—But Structure

January has been misrepresented.

Every year, it is sold as a month of motivation—new energy, fresh willpower, bold resolutions, and emotional reinvention. Yet for millions of people, January does not arrive with momentum. It arrives cold, quiet, and constrained. Bills remain. Systems remain. Limitations remain. The calendar flips, but life does not magically reset.

For those starting with limited resources, motivation is not only unreliable—it is irrelevant.

This book begins with a different premise: **wealth is not created by motivation; it is created by structure**. Motivation spikes and collapses. Structure persists. Motivation demands energy you may not have. Structure conserves energy you cannot afford to waste.

Cold Start Wealth is written for people beginning from a standing still point—those without spare capital, insider access, inherited advantages, or safety nets. It is for readers who are not "behind," but rather **outside the traditional wealth on-ramp**, attempting to move forward without the fuel most financial advice assumes.

In technology, a "cold start" describes a system that must function before it has data, users, or momentum. It cannot wait for scale to work—it must be **designed to produce momentum from zero**. Wealth works the same way. When resources are limited, the only viable strategy is not accumulation, but **momentum design**.

This book reframes wealth creation away from saving fantasies, overnight breakthroughs, or inspirational narratives. Instead, it focuses on **repeatable systems**—small, controllable actions arranged so that movement becomes inevitable, even when motivation fades.

January matters not because it is inspiring, but because it is neutral. It exposes what already exists. Cold weather strips away illusion. Financial reality becomes visible. This is not a month for emotional promises; it is a month for **structural alignment**.

You will not be asked to "believe harder," think positively, or manifest outcomes without mechanisms. You will be asked to observe friction, identify bottlenecks, and construct systems that function under stress. Wealth, in this framework, is not a reward—it is a **byproduct of designed motion**.

Throughout this book, you will explore how momentum can be engineered when time is tight, money is scarce, and attention is fragmented. You will learn how to build financial power not by waiting to feel ready, but by **creating conditions that make progress unavoidable**.

If you are starting with limited resources, this is not a disadvantage—it is a design constraint. And constraints, when understood, are powerful.

January is not asking you to be motivated.

January is asking you to be structured.

This book shows you how.

Chapter 1: The Standing Still Myth

Standing Still Is Not the Same as Doing Nothing

Feeling stuck is commonly interpreted as inactivity, laziness, or lack of effort. In reality, most people who feel "stuck" are expending enormous amounts of energy just to maintain their current position. Bills are paid. Obligations are met. Crises are managed. Life continues to demand motion, even when progress feels absent. The sensation of standing still is not proof of inaction—it is evidence of **energy being consumed without producing forward movement**.

This distinction matters. Doing nothing implies absence of effort. Standing still usually means effort is being applied in ways that cancel themselves out. Energy leaks into maintenance tasks, emotional regulation, and survival decisions that prevent collapse but do not generate momentum. From the outside, this looks like stagnation. From the inside, it feels exhausting.

Wealth advice often ignores this reality. It assumes spare capacity—extra time, extra money, extra focus. When those reserves do not exist, the advice fails, and the reader internalizes the failure. The problem is not effort. The problem is **misaligned effort**.

Standing still, then, is not a personal flaw. It is a system condition. When outputs equal inputs, motion disappears. Recognizing this reframes the problem from "What's wrong with me?" to "What is this system producing?"

Once you see standing still as a system state rather than a personal verdict, shame loosens its grip. You are not broken. You are operating inside a structure that produces equilibrium instead of growth. And structures can be redesigned.

Why Willpower Collapses in Poorly Designed Systems

Willpower is treated as a renewable resource. It is not. It is finite, fragile, and easily depleted by stress, decision fatigue, and uncertainty. Systems that rely on constant motivation inevitably fail—not because people are weak, but because **biology has limits**.

When a system requires daily heroism just to function, collapse is inevitable. Financial advice that demands perfect discipline, consistent optimism, and relentless hustle ignores how humans actually operate under pressure. The more constrained your life, the faster willpower burns out.

This is why January motivation spikes and February collapses. Motivation is being used as fuel instead of structure. When fuel runs out, motion stops. Then shame steps in to explain the halt as personal failure.

A well-designed system assumes low energy days. It anticipates distraction, fatigue, and emotional drag. It does not require you to feel powerful; it **creates power through arrangement**. Willpower becomes a bonus, not a prerequisite.

Understanding this is liberating. You are not failing because you lack drive. You are struggling because your current setup requires more psychological output than is sustainable. Redesign replaces self-blame with strategy.

The Hidden Cost of Maintenance Loops

Maintenance loops are activities that keep life from getting worse but never allow it to get better. Paying minimum balances. Catching up instead of getting ahead. Solving the same problems repeatedly. These loops consume time, money, and attention without compounding returns.

Most people underestimate how much of their life is spent inside these loops. They feel busy, overwhelmed, and constantly behind, yet nothing structurally changes. The system is working exactly as designed—to preserve the current state.

Maintenance loops are not optional. They are necessary for survival. The mistake is believing that maintenance automatically leads to progress. It does not. Without intentional design, maintenance crowds out momentum entirely.

This is why standing still feels like effort without reward. The system absorbs everything you put into it. No surplus remains to generate movement. Wealth creation begins not by eliminating maintenance, but by **isolating it from momentum-building actions**.

Once maintenance is contained, even small momentum structures can begin to operate. Progress does not require escape from responsibility—it requires boundaries around it.

Motion Requires Asymmetry

Standing still occurs when inputs and outputs are balanced. Motion requires asymmetry—something uneven, biased, or tilted in your favor. Traditional advice seeks balance. Momentum requires **imbalance**.

Asymmetry can be tiny. One action that compounds while others remain static. One decision that reduces friction permanently. One system that produces output repeatedly without proportional input. These are leverage points.

When resources are limited, symmetry is a trap. Equal effort across all areas produces exhaustion, not growth. Asymmetry concentrates effort where it multiplies instead of dissipates.

This chapter is not about doing more. It is about doing **differently**. Standing still ends the moment one part of the system begins producing excess. That excess becomes fuel.

You do not need to move everything forward. You need to move **one thing** forward in a way that does not reset overnight.

Identity Damage Is a System Side Effect

Prolonged standing still does not just affect finances—it corrodes identity. People internalize stagnation as evidence of inadequacy. Confidence erodes. Risk tolerance shrinks. Vision narrows to survival.

This identity damage is not inherent. It is a side effect of systems that provide no feedback loops for progress. When effort yields no visible result, the mind concludes that effort is pointless.

This is dangerous, because it disconnects action from outcome. Once that link breaks, even good opportunities feel unreal or undeserved. The system has trained the person to expect cancellation, not reward.

Restoring identity does not require affirmations. It requires **designed wins**—small, repeatable confirmations that action leads somewhere. Systems heal identity by producing evidence.

When structure changes, self-perception follows. Confidence is not summoned; it is rebuilt through feedback.

Standing Still Ends When Design Begins

The standing still myth survives because it personalizes a structural problem. It tells people they are stuck because they are not trying hard enough. In truth, most are trying too hard inside the wrong architecture.

Design is the turning point. The moment you stop asking for more motivation and start asking for better structure, movement becomes possible. Not dramatic movement—reliable movement.

This book does not ask you to leap forward. It asks you to **stop cancelling your own effort**. To redirect energy so that some portion of it survives the day and returns tomorrow.

Standing still is not your identity. It is a signal. And signals exist to be read, not obeyed.

Exercise 1: Mapping the Standing Still Loop

Purpose: Identify where effort is being consumed without producing progress.

Steps:

1. Write down everything you did yesterday related to money, work, or survival.
2. Circle actions that had to be repeated today.
3. Highlight any action that produced a lasting result.
4. Notice how many actions disappear without trace.
5. Write one sentence describing what your system is designed to preserve.

Exercise 2: Effort-to-Outcome Audit
Purpose: Separate effort from effectiveness.
Steps:

1. List three things you work hardest at.
2. For each, write the tangible outcome it produces.
3. Rate the outcome on a scale of 1–10 for long-term impact.
4. Identify one high-effort, low-impact item.
5. Write one way to reduce or contain it.

Exercise 3: Designing a Single Asymmetry
Purpose: Create one non-cancelling action.
Steps:

1. Choose one activity that could compound over time.
2. Define the smallest repeatable version of it.
3. Remove one obstacle that makes it hard to repeat.
4. Schedule it in a low-friction time slot.
5. Commit to consistency, not intensity.

Meditation: The Stillness Scan
Purpose: Reframe stillness as information, not judgment.
Steps:

1. Sit comfortably and close your eyes.
2. Take five slow breaths, extending the exhale.
3. Notice where your body feels heavy or paused.
4. Say silently: "This is information, not failure."
5. Visualize one small movement beginning.
6. Rest with that image for two minutes.
7. Open your eyes slowly.

Journal Prompts

1. Where do I confuse exhaustion with laziness?
2. What effort in my life produces nothing lasting?
3. How has standing still affected my self-image?
4. What would change if I blamed systems instead of myself?
5. Where do I see maintenance masquerading as progress?
6. What is one area where imbalance could help me?
7. What kind of feedback do I currently lack?
8. When did I first start feeling "stuck"?
9. What evidence do I have that effort can work?
10. What would movement look like at 1% scale?

Closing Reflection

Standing still is not a verdict on your worth, intelligence, or discipline. It is a message from a system that has reached equilibrium. Nothing is wrong—you are simply operating inside a design that preserves the present instead of building the future.

This chapter asks you to release the myth that being stuck means being broken. The moment you shift from self-judgment to structural awareness, movement becomes possible. Not through force, but through design.

Progress does not begin when you feel ready.
It begins when the system stops cancelling you.

And that redesign starts now.

Chapter 2: Micro-Leverage

Why Big Effort Fails and Small Systems Survive

Most financial burnout does not come from failure—it comes from **overreach**. People attempt to solve long-term problems with short bursts of extreme effort. They sprint, exhaust themselves, and then collapse back to baseline. The cycle repeats, and each repetition reinforces the belief that consistency is impossible.

Micro-leverage begins by rejecting the idea that progress requires scale. Scale is a *result*, not a requirement. When effort is oversized relative to capacity, it drains emotional and cognitive reserves faster than results can replenish them. Burnout is not a weakness—it is a predictable outcome of mismatched effort.

Small systems survive because they respect reality. They fit into constrained lives. They function on low energy days. They do not require dramatic mood shifts or ideal conditions. They work *because* they are modest, not in spite of it.

A micro-system does not ask, "How fast can I grow?" It asks, "What can I repeat even when everything else is heavy?" That question alone filters out most self-sabotaging strategies.

Wealth does not begin with ambition. It begins with **what you can sustain without self-betrayal**.

Leverage Is Not Force—It Is Placement

Leverage is often misunderstood as doing more with less effort. In reality, leverage is about **placing effort where it multiplies** instead of evaporates. Two identical actions can have radically different outcomes depending on where they sit in the system.

Micro-leverage focuses on placement, not intensity. It looks for actions that create secondary effects: learning that improves future decisions, outputs that persist, or habits that reduce friction later. These actions may feel unimpressive in the moment, but their impact grows quietly.

Force tries to overpower resistance. Placement sidesteps it. This is why micro-leverage does not feel heroic—it feels almost anticlimactic. Yet over time, it outpaces force-based effort because it does not provoke exhaustion or resistance.

When leverage is correct, progress feels oddly calm. You are not pushing uphill; you are adjusting angles. Energy is conserved, not consumed.

The goal is not to feel powerful today, but to **be stronger next month without trying harder**.

Burnout Is a Signal of Poor Return on Energy

Burnout is often framed as emotional overload, but at its core, it is a **return-on-energy problem**. When energy spent does not produce meaningful or lasting results, the nervous system resists further effort.

Micro-leverage restores trust between effort and outcome. It creates systems where small inputs reliably produce visible outputs. This rebuilds confidence—not as a belief, but as a lived experience.

If an action must be repeated at full cost every time, it is not leveraged. True leverage lowers the cost of repetition. Templates, routines, automation, and constraints all serve this function. They reduce the *price* of action.

Burnout fades when effort begins to echo. When something you do today makes tomorrow easier, motivation becomes unnecessary. The system pulls you forward.

This is why micro-leverage is protective. It prevents overexertion by design.

Compounding Is Quiet and Unemotional

Compounding is often romanticized as exponential growth. In practice, it feels boring. Uneventful. Sometimes invisible. This is why many abandon compounding systems before they mature—they mistake quiet for failure.

Micro-leverage embraces this quiet phase. It assumes that early progress will be subtle. The reward is not immediate payoff, but **future reduction of effort**. Less friction. Fewer decisions. Faster execution.

Compounding works because it stacks advantage incrementally. Skills improve. Processes refine. Confidence stabilizes. None of this announces itself loudly.

If you require emotional reinforcement to continue, compounding will fail. Micro-leverage systems are designed to operate even when enthusiasm is absent. They rely on structure, not excitement.

The true signal of compounding is not speed—it is **ease**.

Designing for Low Energy Days

Most systems are built for ideal conditions. Micro-leverage is built for **worst-case scenarios**. It assumes fatigue, distraction, stress, and limited time. If a system only works when you feel good, it does not work.

Designing for low energy means reducing steps, lowering thresholds, and removing optional complexity. The system must be executable on your worst reasonable day, not your best.

This does not mean lowering standards. It means lowering friction. High standards paired with low friction create consistency. High standards paired with high friction create abandonment.

Micro-leverage systems are humble. They do not impress others. They protect you.

If you can perform the system when you are tired, the system will compound when you are strong.

Micro-Leverage Turns Time into an Ally

When effort is oversized, time becomes an enemy. Deadlines loom. Delays feel catastrophic. Missed days feel like failure. Micro-leverage reverses this relationship.

Because the system is small, time works *for* you. Each repetition adds marginal advantage. Missing a day does not collapse progress. Returning does not require recovery.

This resilience is crucial. Wealth is built over time, not through perfect streaks. Micro-leverage tolerates imperfection without resetting to zero.

When time stops threatening you, momentum becomes possible. You are no longer racing—you are **accumulating**.

And accumulation, quietly and patiently, changes everything.

Exercise 1: Energy-to-Return Mapping
Purpose: Identify actions that drain energy without compounding.
Steps:

1. List five recurring actions related to money or work.
2. Note the energy cost of each (low, medium, high).
3. Identify the lasting outcome each produces.
4. Cross out any high-cost, low-return action.
5. Write one way to reduce its cost or frequency.

Exercise 2: Designing a One-Minute System
Purpose: Create a system that survives low energy.
Steps:

1. Choose one wealth-related habit.
2. Reduce it to a one-minute version.
3. Remove all optional steps.
4. Decide when it will occur.
5. Commit to repetition, not expansion.

Exercise 3: Leveraged Placement Test
Purpose: Improve placement of effort.
Steps:

1. Choose one small action you already take.
2. Ask how its output could persist.
3. Modify it so it creates a reusable result.
4. Test the change for one week.
5. Observe whether effort feels lighter.

Meditation: The Compounding Breath
Purpose: Anchor patience and reduce urgency.
Steps:

1. Sit comfortably and close your eyes.
2. Inhale slowly for four counts.
3. Exhale slowly for six counts.
4. With each exhale, imagine effort spreading forward in time.
5. Repeat for five minutes.
6. End by reminding yourself: “Small builds strong.”

Journal Prompts

1. Where do I overexert instead of redesign?
2. Which actions exhaust me without payoff?
3. What would sustainability look like for me?
4. How do I react to slow progress?
5. What small action could compound quietly?
6. Where can I reduce friction immediately?
7. What system would survive my worst day?
8. How do I measure progress emotionally?
9. What does ease signal to me?
10. How could time become my ally?

Closing Reflection

Micro-leverage rejects the myth that success requires constant intensity. It proves that small, well-placed systems outperform heroic effort over time. When leverage is correct, progress no longer demands sacrifice—it emerges naturally.

This chapter invites you to stop forcing growth and start **designing for endurance**. Wealth is not built by burning bright and burning out. It is built by systems that keep going when enthusiasm fades.

Small does not mean weak.

Quiet does not mean stagnant.

When effort compounds without draining you, momentum becomes inevitable—and burnout loses its power.

Chapter 3: Energy-Based Budgeting

Why Money Fails When Energy Is Ignored

Traditional budgeting treats money as an isolated variable. Income comes in, expenses go out, and whatever remains is judged as success or failure. This model assumes that time and energy are unlimited, stable, and irrelevant. In real life, they are not. When energy collapses, financial plans collapse with it.

Energy is the hidden currency behind every financial decision. Attention determines what you notice. Time determines what you can execute. Energy determines what you can sustain. Ignoring these forces creates budgets that look good on paper and fail in practice.

Many people believe they are bad with money when the real issue is **energy mismatch**. They attempt to manage finances during periods of exhaustion, distraction, or stress. Decisions made in low-energy states are often reactive, short-term, and costly.

Energy-based budgeting reframes financial management as a system that must align with human capacity. Instead of asking, "What should I do with my money?" it asks, "What can I reliably manage with the energy I actually have?"

When budgets respect energy, consistency becomes possible. And consistency, not perfection, is what compounds.

Attention Is the First Budget

Before money is spent, attention is spent. What you focus on shapes what you value, worry about, and prioritize. If attention is constantly fragmented, financial decisions become scattered and impulsive.

Modern life aggressively competes for attention. Notifications, media, obligations, and stress consume mental bandwidth long before a dollar is spent. This leaves little capacity for thoughtful financial planning.

Energy-based budgeting treats attention as the first line item. If you do not control where your focus goes, your money will follow chaos. Clarity begins not with spreadsheets, but with **protected mental space.**

This does not require extreme discipline. It requires intentional narrowing. Fewer financial decisions, fewer tracking points, fewer priorities. Attention conserved is energy preserved.

When attention is stabilized, better decisions follow naturally.

Time Is a Constraint, Not a Resource

Time is often described as something to "find" or "make." In reality, time is a fixed boundary. You cannot create more of it—you can only decide how it is consumed.

Energy-based budgeting recognizes that every financial action requires time. Tracking expenses, researching options, managing accounts—all of these have time costs that are rarely acknowledged.

Overcomplicated financial systems fail because they demand ongoing time investments that exceed capacity. The result is avoidance, guilt, and eventual abandonment.

A sustainable system fits within the time you realistically control. It favors automation, batching, and simplification. It does not require constant monitoring or frequent decision-making.

When time demands shrink, follow-through improves. The best budget is the one that survives your actual schedule.

Energy Determines Financial Behavior

Energy levels directly influence spending, saving, and planning. Low energy increases impulsivity. High energy supports foresight. Ignoring this leads to moralizing behavior that is actually physiological.

Many financial "mistakes" occur when energy is depleted. Convenience spending, emotional purchases, and avoidance are not character flaws—they are predictable responses to fatigue.

Energy-based budgeting anticipates these patterns. It builds guardrails for low-energy moments rather than pretending they will not happen. This might include simplifying choices, reducing access to temptation, or scheduling financial decisions during peak energy windows.

By aligning financial behavior with energy cycles, you reduce friction and self-blame. The system supports you instead of fighting you.

When energy is respected, discipline becomes less necessary.

Integrating Money, Time, and Attention

Traditional budgets track money alone. Energy-based budgets track **interactions**. A low-cost choice that consumes massive time or attention may be more expensive than a higher-cost option that frees capacity.

This perspective shifts decision-making. Instead of asking, "Is this cheaper?" you ask, "What does this cost me in energy?" Sometimes paying more is the more sustainable choice.

Integration also reveals hidden leaks. Tasks that drain attention create financial errors. Time pressure leads to rushed decisions. Energy depletion leads to avoidance.

By viewing money, time, and attention as a single system, you begin to see where imbalance occurs. Corrections become strategic rather than reactive.

Wealth grows when all three move in alignment.

Budgets That Heal Instead of Punish

Many budgets fail because they are punitive. They assume discipline must be enforced through restriction and guilt. Energy-based budgeting replaces punishment with **design**.

A healing budget reduces decision load. It accommodates fluctuations. It forgives mistakes without collapsing. It is resilient, not rigid.

This approach builds trust. When you stop fighting yourself, consistency returns. Progress may be slower, but it is stable.

A budget that respects energy becomes a supportive structure rather than a source of stress. It creates safety, and safety enables growth.

Wealth is not built by deprivation—it is built by systems that allow you to function.

Exercise 1: Energy Expense Audit
Purpose: Identify where energy is being overspent.
Steps:

1. List five recurring financial tasks.
2. Rate the energy cost of each.
3. Identify which feel most draining.
4. Note which tasks could be simplified.
5. Choose one to redesign.

Exercise 2: Attention Budget Design
Purpose: Protect mental bandwidth.
Steps:

1. Choose one daily time window for financial attention.
2. Limit financial decisions to that window.
3. Remove financial apps or alerts outside it.
4. Observe stress levels for one week.
5. Adjust as needed.

Exercise 3: Low-Energy Safeguards
Purpose: Prevent poor decisions during fatigue.
Steps:

1. Identify one low-energy spending pattern.
2. Create a barrier or delay.
3. Prepare an alternative action.
4. Test during the next low-energy moment.
5. Reflect on the outcome.

Meditation: The Resource Alignment Pause
Purpose: Reconnect money decisions with capacity.
Steps:

1. Sit quietly and close your eyes.
2. Take five slow breaths.
3. Visualize time, attention, and money as streams.
4. Imagine them aligning smoothly.
5. Sit with the image for three minutes.
6. Open your eyes gently.

Journal Prompts

1. Where do I spend energy without noticing?
2. How does fatigue affect my financial choices?
3. What financial task do I avoid most?
4. Where could simplicity help me?
5. How do I react to restrictive budgets?
6. What would a supportive budget feel like?
7. When am I most mentally clear?
8. How could I protect that time?
9. What decision load can I remove?
10. How does alignment change my view of wealth?

Closing Reflection

Energy-based budgeting is not about control—it is about respect. When you acknowledge that attention, time, and money are interconnected, financial management becomes humane instead of harsh.

This chapter invites you to stop treating exhaustion as a personal failure and start designing systems that work with your capacity. Wealth grows best in environments where energy is protected, not punished.

When your budget honors how you actually live,
progress stops feeling like resistance
and starts feeling like relief.

Chapter 4: Income Without Identity Collapse

Why Income Pressure Fractures Identity

Income is rarely just financial. It carries emotional weight, social meaning, and identity pressure. When money is scarce, income becomes loaded with fear. When opportunities appear, they often demand compromise. This is where identity collapse begins—not because people lack values, but because **systems reward disconnection**.

Many revenue strategies require becoming someone else: louder, harsher, more performative, less honest. Over time, this creates a split between who you are and how you earn. That split drains energy faster than low income ever could.

Identity collapse does not happen all at once. It accumulates quietly through small betrayals—accepting work that feels wrong, presenting a version of yourself that is unsustainable, or tying self-worth entirely to output. Money comes in, but coherence leaks out.

This chapter begins with a refusal: income does not have to cost you your sense of self. Revenue built on self-erasure is unstable. It requires constant emotional labor just to maintain.

Sustainable income supports identity instead of consuming it. Anything else is a temporary fix with long-term consequences.

The Hidden Cost of Performative Earning

Performative earning occurs when income depends on constant presentation—selling a persona, maintaining visibility, or projecting certainty you do not feel. While this can work short-term, it creates chronic stress.

Performance requires energy beyond the task itself. You must manage perception, tone, timing, and response. Over time, this doubles the workload without doubling the return.

The danger is subtle. What begins as adaptation becomes habit. Eventually, you forget where the performance ends and you begin. This erosion is often misdiagnosed as burnout or lack of motivation.

Income streams that demand ongoing emotional performance are expensive. They tax attention, drain authenticity, and create fragility. One bad day, one misstep, and the system wobbles.

Income without identity collapse minimizes performance. It favors **function over persona**.

Revenue That Respects Your Nervous System

Your nervous system is part of your financial infrastructure. Income sources that require constant urgency, conflict, or unpredictability keep the body in a state of alert. This limits creativity, foresight, and resilience.

Energy-based income design asks a different question: "Can my body tolerate this repeatedly?" If the answer is no, the income is not sustainable—regardless of payout.

Revenue that respects the nervous system tends to be quieter. It may be slower initially, but it compounds because it does not provoke avoidance. You do not need to psych yourself up to engage with it.

This does not mean avoiding challenge. It means avoiding **chronic threat**. There is a difference between growth discomfort and identity danger.

Income that allows regulation creates longevity. Longevity creates wealth.

Separating Worth from Output

One of the most destructive financial patterns is tying self-worth directly to income. When revenue fluctuates—as it always does—identity swings with it. Confidence becomes conditional.

This creates emotional volatility. Good months feel euphoric. Slow months feel existential. Decision-making becomes reactive, driven by fear rather than strategy.

Income without identity collapse requires separation. You are not your numbers. Revenue is feedback, not judgment. When this boundary is clear, income becomes easier to manage.

Detachment does not mean indifference. It means stability. You can care about results without letting them define you.

When worth is stable, income strategies become cleaner and more effective.

Designing Revenue That Fits Your Shape

Most income advice is generic. It assumes interchangeable people. In reality, each person has a specific shape—energy patterns, tolerance levels, communication styles, and constraints.

Income systems fail when they ignore this shape. People force themselves into models that look good externally but feel wrong internally. The result is resistance and eventual abandonment.

Designing income that fits you means honoring limitations instead of fighting them. It means choosing models that align with how you think, work, and recover.

This is not about comfort—it is about compatibility. Systems that fit require less force. Less force means less burnout.

Revenue built in alignment compounds quietly.

Income as Infrastructure, Not Identity

The final reframe is simple but powerful: income is infrastructure. It supports life; it does not define it. Roads do not become the destination. They enable movement.

When income is treated as infrastructure, decisions become pragmatic instead of emotional. You evaluate sources based on stability, cost, and maintenance—not validation.

This shift removes drama. You can adjust, replace, or pause income streams without personal crisis. Flexibility increases.

Wealth grows fastest when income is boring, reliable, and identity-neutral. The quieter the system, the stronger it becomes.

Income should serve your life—not consume it.

Exercise 1: Identity Cost Assessment
Purpose: Identify income-related self-betrayal.
Steps:

1. List all current or recent income sources.
2. Note how each makes you feel emotionally.
3. Identify any that require ongoing performance.
4. Mark any that drain your sense of self.
5. Choose one to modify or replace.

Exercise 2: Nervous System Check-In
Purpose: Align income with capacity.
Steps:

1. Think about one income activity.
2. Notice your body's response.
3. Rate stress from 1–10.
4. Identify the source of stress.
5. Write one way to reduce it.

Exercise 3: Revenue Without Persona
Purpose: Reduce performative earning.
Steps:

1. Choose one income-related task.
2. Remove unnecessary presentation.
3. Simplify communication.
4. Automate or template where possible.
5. Observe energy levels after one week.

Meditation: The Boundary Reset
Purpose: Separate worth from income.
Steps:

1. Sit comfortably and close your eyes.
2. Breathe slowly for one minute.
3. Repeat silently: “My worth is stable.”
4. Visualize income as a neutral tool.
5. Sit with the image for three minutes.
6. Open your eyes gently.

Journal Prompts

1. Where have I betrayed myself for money?
2. What income feels most draining?
3. How do I perform to earn?
4. What would income look like without performance?
5. How does stress show up in my body?
6. What income supports regulation?
7. Where do I confuse worth with results?
8. What revenue fits my real capacity?
9. How could income feel quieter?
10. What would change if money were infrastructure?

Closing Reflection

Income should not require you to disappear. When earning demands self-erasure, the cost is too high—even if the numbers look good.

This chapter invites you to build revenue that respects who you are, how you function, and what you can sustain. Wealth created through self-betrayal eventually collapses under its own weight.

Income built with integrity endures.
Income built with alignment compounds.

When money supports identity instead of consuming it,
financial power becomes stable—and so do you.

Chapter 5: Cold Start Scaling

Why Traditional Scaling Advice Breaks Cold Starts

Most scaling advice assumes momentum already exists. It presumes spare capital, stable income, emotional bandwidth, and margin for error. For cold starts—where resources are limited and systems are fragile—this advice is not just unhelpful, it is dangerous.

Traditional scaling encourages expansion before stabilization. More products. More platforms. More exposure. More spending. Each addition increases complexity, risk, and cognitive load. For someone starting from stillness, this creates overload long before growth appears.

Cold start scaling rejects the idea that growth must be aggressive to be real. It recognizes that **premature expansion amplifies weakness**. If a system cannot survive at small scale, scaling it only multiplies the damage.

This chapter reframes scaling as a structural process, not a volume increase. Growth begins by making the system stronger, not bigger.

The goal is not speed—it is survivability.

Risk Is Cumulative, Not Isolated

Risk is rarely a single decision. It accumulates quietly through overlapping commitments, obligations, and dependencies. Each new initiative adds a layer of exposure that must be managed.

Cold starts are especially vulnerable to cumulative risk. One missed payment, one failed launch, or one burnout episode can destabilize the entire structure. This makes traditional "all-in" strategies reckless.

Cold start scaling treats risk like weight. You do not add load until the structure can bear it. This requires patience and restraint—qualities often mistaken for fear.

Reducing risk does not mean avoiding growth. It means sequencing growth so that **each step reduces vulnerability** instead of increasing it.

When risk is managed intentionally, confidence grows organically.

Scaling Systems Before Scaling Output

The safest way to scale is to strengthen systems before increasing demand. This means refining processes, simplifying workflows, and reducing dependency on peak energy or constant attention.

Systems that require manual effort at every stage do not scale—they strain. Cold start scaling prioritizes repeatability. What can be done the same way every time? What can be templated, automated, or constrained?

Scaling systems also means testing failure. What happens if you miss a day? A week? Does everything collapse, or does the system hold?

A scalable system is resilient. It absorbs fluctuation without breaking. Output comes later.

This inversion—systems first, volume second—is the foundation of safe growth.

Incremental Expansion and Contained Bets

Cold start scaling favors small, contained bets over large, irreversible commitments. Each expansion is limited in scope, cost, and downside. If it fails, recovery is possible.

This approach turns scaling into a series of experiments rather than a single leap. Feedback is gathered. Adjustments are made. Confidence increases without risking collapse.

Contained bets protect identity as well as finances. Failure does not feel catastrophic because it was anticipated and bounded. This reduces fear-driven decision-making.

Growth becomes a conversation with reality instead of a confrontation.

When expansion is incremental, learning compounds alongside revenue.

The Role of Timing in Risk Management

Timing is a form of leverage. Scaling at the wrong moment—even with a good idea—can create unnecessary stress. Cold start scaling emphasizes readiness over urgency.

Readiness is not about perfection. It is about **stability under current conditions**. Are your systems consistent? Is your energy predictable? Are your finances buffered, even slightly?

Scaling too early often comes from impatience or comparison. Scaling too late often comes from fear. Cold start scaling finds the middle path by listening to system signals.

When timing is aligned, scaling feels less like a gamble and more like a progression.

Growth that respects timing preserves momentum.

Growth Without Identity Erosion

Scaling often threatens identity. More exposure means more judgment. More income means more pressure. Without boundaries, growth can undo the coherence built earlier.

Cold start scaling protects identity by maintaining constraints. You do not scale everything. You scale what fits. You say no to growth that demands self-erasure.

This selective expansion keeps the system humane. You remain recognizable to yourself even as output increases.

Wealth built without identity erosion is stable. It does not require constant recalibration or recovery.

Growth that costs you yourself is not growth—it is extraction.

Exercise 1: Risk Layer Mapping
Purpose: Identify cumulative risk.
Steps:

1. List current commitments.
2. Note financial, time, and energy costs.
3. Identify overlapping stress points.
4. Highlight any fragile dependencies.
5. Choose one risk to reduce.

Exercise 2: System Stress Test
Purpose: Evaluate scalability.
Steps:

1. Choose one system.
2. Simulate a low-output week.
3. Observe what breaks.
4. Identify reinforcement points.
5. Strengthen one element.

Exercise 3: Contained Expansion Plan
Purpose: Design safe growth.
Steps:

1. Identify one expansion idea.
2. Limit cost and scope.
3. Define a clear stop point.
4. Set a review date.
5. Execute cautiously.

Meditation: The Steady Growth Visualization
Purpose: Reduce urgency.
Steps:

1. Sit comfortably and close your eyes.
2. Breathe slowly for two minutes.
3. Visualize growth unfolding gradually.
4. Notice stability at each stage.
5. Sit with calm confidence.
6. Open your eyes gently.

Journal Prompts

1. Where have I rushed growth?
2. What risks do I carry silently?
3. How does scaling affect my stress?
4. What system needs strengthening?
5. How do I react to slow growth?
6. What expansion feels aligned?
7. Where can I reduce exposure?
8. How do I define readiness?
9. What growth preserves identity?
10. What does sustainable scaling mean to me?

Closing Reflection

Cold start scaling is not about restraint—it is about intelligence. It recognizes that growth is only valuable if it can be carried without collapse.

This chapter invites you to grow in a way that respects your limits, protects your identity, and manages risk deliberately. Wealth built slowly but securely outlasts growth built on pressure.

You do not need to gamble to grow.
You need systems that can hold more—
without breaking you.

When scaling honors structure,
progress becomes steady, safe, and real.

Appendix A: The Cold Start Blueprint

This appendix is designed to be **used**, not admired. It is not a philosophy, mindset exercise, or motivational framework. It is a **practical system map** for moments when momentum is absent, energy is constrained, and progress feels inaccessible.

The Cold Start Blueprint exists for one reason:
to create **movement without requiring motivation**.

It assumes:

- limited resources
- inconsistent energy
- high cognitive load
- emotional fatigue
- no existing momentum

And it works anyway.

Phase 1: Stabilize Before You Optimize

Goal: Stop internal and external collapse before attempting growth.

Zero-momentum phases are dangerous not because nothing is happening, but because **systems are fragile**. The first mistake most people make is trying to improve before stabilizing.

Stabilization is about **reducing volatility**, not increasing performance.

Step 1: Identify Non-Negotiables

Write down what must continue functioning for life not to get worse:

- housing
- food
- utilities
- minimum income
- basic health

This list is usually smaller than you think. Everything else is optional during cold start mode.

Step 2: Freeze Expansion

No new projects.
No new obligations.
No new complexity.

Cold starts require **containment**. Expansion during fragility multiplies risk.

Step 3: Lower the Operating Baseline

Redefine "a good day" as **maintenance without damage**.
Progress comes later.

Stability is success at this stage.

Phase 2: Map Energy, Not Ambition

Goal: Align action with capacity instead of desire.
Ambition lies during cold starts. Energy tells the truth.

Step 4: Create an Energy Inventory

For three days, observe:

- when energy rises
- when it crashes
- what drains it fastest
- what restores it

Do not judge. Just record.

Step 5: Define Your Low-Energy Default

Design systems that function at **60% capacity** or less.
If a task requires full alertness, it does not belong in cold start mode.

Step 6: Assign Tasks to Energy States

- high energy → creation
- medium energy → organization
- low energy → maintenance or rest

This prevents self-sabotage through mistiming.

Phase 3: Contain Maintenance Loops

Goal: Stop survival tasks from consuming all momentum.

Maintenance is necessary—but unbounded maintenance kills progress.

Step 7: Box Maintenance

Choose specific times for:

- bills
- admin
- errands
- emotional labor

Outside those boxes, maintenance is **off-limits**.

Step 8: Reduce Frequency
Ask:

- Can this be done weekly instead of daily?
- Can it be automated?
- Can it be simplified?

Every reduction frees energy.

Step 9: Separate Maintenance From Growth
Never attempt growth tasks immediately after maintenance. They use different mental systems.

Phase 4: Install a Single Momentum Engine

Goal: Create one repeatable action that does not reset.

Cold starts fail when people attempt multiple engines. One is enough.

Step 10: Choose a Compounding Action

Criteria:

- produces lasting output
- low energy to repeat
- survivable on bad days
- emotionally neutral

Examples include writing, asset creation, skill accumulation, or system building.

Step 11: Shrink It Below Comfort

Make it so small it feels almost trivial.
The goal is **non-cancellation**, not speed.

Step 12: Lock the Placement

Same time. Same context. Same trigger.
Consistency creates momentum without effort.

Phase 5: Add Friction Where It Protects You

Goal: Prevent energy leaks and impulsive damage.
Not all friction is bad. Some friction saves you.

Step 13: Block High-Cost Behaviors
Add delays to:

- impulsive spending
- reactive decisions
- emotional commitments

Cold starts require guardrails.

Step 14: Remove Friction From Momentum Tasks
No setup.
No decision.
No negotiation.
If starting feels heavy, redesign.

Phase 6: Measure Stability, Not Speed

Goal: Track what matters in zero-momentum phases.
Speed metrics create shame. Stability metrics create progress.

Step 15: Track Only Three Signals

- system consistency
- energy preservation
- identity alignment

Revenue and scale come later.

Step 16: Review Weekly, Not Daily

Daily reviews magnify noise.
Weekly reviews reveal trends.

Phase 7: Expand Only When Pressure Drops

Goal: Scale without risk overload.
Growth begins when effort feels lighter—not heavier.

Step 17: Watch for Expansion Signals

- tasks feel easier
- energy rebounds faster
- systems run without vigilance

These are green lights.

Step 18: Add One Variable at a Time

Never expand more than one dimension simultaneously.
Capacity must precede complexity.

Phase 8: Reset Without Shame

Goal: Prevent collapse after interruption.
Cold starts recur. This is normal.

Step 19: Design Restart Points
Know exactly where to resume after disruption.
No "starting over." Only **continuing**.

Step 20: Re-enter Through the Smallest Door
Momentum returns faster when re-entry is easy.

Final Integration: The Cold Start Loop

When momentum disappears:

1. stabilize
2. map energy
3. contain maintenance
4. run one engine
5. protect capacity
6. measure stability
7. expand cautiously
8. reset gently

This loop is repeatable at any stage of life.

Closing Reflection

Zero-momentum phases are not failures—they are **transitions**. They demand different rules, different metrics, and different expectations.

The Cold Start Blueprint exists to keep you moving when motivation is gone, resources are thin, and systems feel heavy. It does not promise speed. It promises **continuity**.

And continuity is enough.

Momentum is not something you wait for.
It is something you design—
one small, survivable step at a time.

Message from the Author:

I hope you enjoyed this book, I love astrology and knew there was not a book such as this out on the shelf. I love metaphysical items as well. Please check out my other books:

-Life of Government Benefits

-My life of Hell

-My life with Hydrocephalus

-Red Sky

-World Domination:Woman's rule

-World Domination:Woman's Rule 2: The War

-Life and Banishment of Apophis: book 1

-The Kidney Friendly Diet

-The Ultimate Hemp Cookbook

-Creating a Dispensary(legally)

-Cleanliness throughout life: the importance of showering from childhood to adulthood.

-Strong Roots: The Risks of Overcoddling children

-Hemp Horoscopes: Cosmic Insights and Earthly Healing

- Celestial Hemp Navigating the Zodiac: Through the Green Cosmos

-Astrological Hemp: Aligning The Stars with Earth's Ancient Herb

-The Astrological Guide to Hemp: Stars, Signs, and Sacred Leaves

-Green Growth: Innovative Marketing Strategies for your Hemp Products and Dispensary

-Cosmic Cannabis

-Astrological Munchies

-Henry The Hemp

-Zodiacal Roots: The Astrological Soul Of Hemp

- **Green Constellations: Intersection of Hemp and Zodiac**

-Hemp in The Houses: An astrological Adventure Through The Cannabis Galaxy

-Galactic Ganja Guide

Heavenly Hemp

Zodiac Leaves

Doctor Who Astrology

Cannastrology

Stellar Satvias and Cosmic Indicas

Celestial Cannabis: A Zodiac Journey

AstroHerbology: The Sky and The Soil: Volume 1

AstroHerbology:Celestial Cannabis:Volume 2

Cosmic Cannabis Cultivation

The Starry Guide to Herbal Harmony: Volume 1

The Starry Guide to Herbal Harmony: Cannabis Universe: Volume 2

Yugioh Astrology: Astrological Guide to Deck, Duels and more

Nightmare Mansion: Echoes of The Abyss

Nightmare Mansion 2: Legacy of Shadows

Nightmare Mansion 3: Shadows of the Forgotten

Nightmare Mansion 4: Echoes of the Damned

The Life and Banishment of Apophis: Book 2

Nightmare Mansion: Halls of Despair

Healing with Herb: Cannabis and Hydrocephalus

Planetary Pot: Aligning with Astrological Herbs: Volume 1

Fast Track to Freedom: 30 Days to Financial Independence Using AI, Assets, and Agile Hustles

Cosmic Hemp Pathways

How to Become Financially Free in 30 Days: 10,000 Paths to Prosperity

Zodiacal Herbage: Astrological Insights: Volume 1

Nightmare Mansion: Whispers in the Walls

The Daleks Invade Atlantis

Henry the hemp and Hydrocephalus

10X The Kidney Friendly Diet

Cannabis Universe: Adult coloring book

Hemp Astrology: The Healing Power of the Stars

Zodiacal Herbage: Astrological Insights: Cannabis Universe: Volume 2

Planetary Pot: Aligning with Astrological Herbs: Cannabis Universes: Volume 2

Doctor Who: Convergence Protocol – The Replicator War

Nightmare Mansion: Curse of the Blood Moon

The Celestial Stoner: A Guide to the Zodiac

Cosmic Pleasures: Sex Toy Astrology for Every Sign

Hydrocephalus Astrology: Navigating the Stars and Healing Waters

Lapis and the Mischievous Chocolate Bar

Celestial Positions: Sexual Astrology for Every Sign

Apophis's Shadow Work Journal: **:** A Journey of Self-Discovery and Healing

Kinky Cosmos: Sexual Kink Astrology for Every Sign

Digital Cosmos: The Astrological Digimon Compendium

Stellar Seeds: The Cosmic Guide to Growing with Astrology

Apophis's Daily Gratitude Journal

Cat Astrology: Feline Mysteries of the Cosmos

The Cosmic Kama Sutra: An Astrological Guide to Sexual Positions

Unleash Your Potential: A Guided Journal Powered by AI Insights

Whispers of the Enchanted Grove

Cosmic Pleasures: An Astrological Guide to Sexual Kinks

369, 12 Manifestation Journal

Whisper of the nocturne journal(blank journal for writing or drawing)

The Boogey Book

Locked In Reflection: A Chastity Journey Through Locktober

Generating Wealth Quickly:How to Generate $100,000 in 24 Hours

Star Magic: Harness the Power of the Universe

The Flatulence Chronicles: A Fart Journal for Self-Discovery

The Doctor and The Death Moth

Seize the Day: A Personal Seizure Tracking Journal

The Ultimate Boogeyman Safari: A Journey into the Boogie World and Beyond

Whispers of Samhain: 1,000 Spells of Love, Luck, and Lunar Magic: Samhain Spell Book

Apophis's guides:Witch's Spellbook Crafting Guide for Halloween

Frost & Flame: The Enchanted Yule Grimoire of 1000 Winter Spells

The Ultimate Boogey Goo Guide & Spooky Activities for Halloween Fun

Harmony of the Scales: A Libra's Spellcraft for Balance and Beauty

The Enchanted Advent: 36 Days of Christmas Wonders

Nightmare Mansion: The Labyrinth of Screams

Harvest of Enchantment: 1,000 Spells of Gratitude, Love, and Fortune for Thanksgiving

The Boogey Chronicles: A Journal of Nightly Encounters and Shadowy Secrets

The 12 Days of Financial Freedom: A Step-by-Step Christmas Countdown to Transform Your Finances

Sigil of the Eternal Spiral Blank Journal

A Christmas Feast: Timeless Recipes for Every Meal

Holiday Stress-Free Solutions: A Survival Guide to Thriving During the Festive Season

Yu-Gi-Oh! Holiday Gifting Mastery: The Ultimate Guide for Fans and Newcomers Alike

Holiday Harmony: A Hydrocephalus Survival Guide for the Festive Season

Celestial Craft: The Witch's Almanac for 2025 – A Cosmic Guide to Manifestations, Moons, and Mystical Events

Doctor Who: The Toymaker's Winter Wonderland

Tulsa King Unveiled: A Thrilling Guide to Stallone's Mafia Masterpiece

Pendulum Craft: A Complete Guide to Crafting and Using Personalized Divination Tools

Nightmare Mansion: Santa's Eternal Eve

Starlight Noel: A Cosmic Journey through Christmas Mysteries

The Dark Architect: Unlocking the Blueprint of Existence

Surviving the Embrace: The Ultimate Guide to Encounters with The Hugging Molly

The Enchanted Codex: Secrets of the Craft for Witches, Wiccans, and Pagans

Harvest of Gratitude: A Complete Thanksgiving Guide

Yuletide Essentials: A Complete Guide to an Authentic and Magical Christmas

Celestial Smokes: A Cosmic Guide to Cigars and Astrology

Living in Balance: A Comprehensive Survival Guide to Thriving with Diabetes Insipidus

Cosmic Symbiosis: The Venom Zodiac Chronicles

The Cursed Paw of Ambition

Cosmic Symbiosis: The Astrological Venom Journal

Celestial Wonders Unfold: A Stargazer's Guide to the Cosmos (2024-2029)

The Ultimate Black Friday Prepper's Guide: Mastering Shopping Strategies and Savings

Cosmic Sales: The Astrological Guide to Black Friday Shopping

Legends of the Corn Mother and Other Harvest Myths

Whispers of the Harvest: The Corn Mother's Journal

The Evergreen Spellbook

The Doctor Meets the Boogeyman

The White Witch of Rose Hall's SpellBook

The Gingerbread Golem's Shadow: A Study in Sweet Darkness

The Gingerbread Golem Codex: An Academic Exploration of Sweet Myths

The Gingerbread Golem Grimoire: Sweet Magicks and Spells for the Festive Witch

The Curse of the Gingerbread Golem

10-minute Christmas Crafts for kids

Christmas Crisis Solutions: The Ultimate Last-Minute Survival Guide

Gingerbread Golem Recipes: Holiday Treats with a Magical Twist

The Infinite Key: Unlocking Mystical Secrets of the Ages

Enchanted Yule: A Wiccan and Pagan Guide to a Magical and Memorable Season

Dinosaurs of Power: Unlocking Ancient Magick

Astro-Dinos: The Cosmic Guide to Prehistoric Wisdom

Gallifrey's Yule Logs: A Festive Doctor Who Cookbook

The Dino Grimoire: Secrets of Prehistoric Magick

The Gift They Never Knew They Needed

The Gingerbread Golem's Culinary Alchemy: Enchanting Recipes for a Sweetly Dark Feast

A Time Lord Christmas: Holiday Adventures with the Doctor

Krampusproofing Your Home: Defensive Strategies for Yule

Silent Frights: A Collection of Christmas Creepypastas to Chill Your Bones

Santa Raptor's Jolly Carnage: A Dino-Claus Christmas Tale

Prehistoric Palettes: A Dino Wicca Coloring Journey

The Christmas Wishkeeper Chronicles

The Starlight Sleigh: A Holiday Journey

Elf Secrets: The True Magic of the North Pole

Candy Cane Conjurations

Cooking with Kids: Recipes Under 20 Minutes

Doctor Who: The TARDIS Confiscation

The Anxiety First Aid Kit: Quick Tools to Calm Your Mind

Frosty Whispers: A Winter's Tale

The Infinite Key: Unlocking the Secrets to Prosperity, Resilience, and Purpose

The Grasping Void: Why You'll Regret This Purchase

Astrology for Busy Bees: Star Signs Simplified

The Instant Focus Formula: Cut Through the Noise

The Secret Language of Colors: Unlocking the Emotional Codes

Sacred Fossil Chronicles: Blank Journal

The Christmas Cottage Miracle

Feeding Frenzy: Graboid-Inspired Recipes

Manifest in Minutes: The Quick Law of Attraction Guide

The Symbiote Chronicles: Doctor Who's Venomous Journey

Think Tiny, Grow Big: The Minimalist Mindset

The Energy Key: Unlocking Limitless Motivation

New Year, New Magic: Manifesting Your Best Year Yet

Unstoppable You: Mastering Confidence in Minutes

Infinite Energy: The Secret to Never Feeling Drained

Lightning Focus: Mastering the Art of Productivity in a Distracted World

Saturnalia Manifestation Magick: A Guide to Unlocking Abundance During the Solstice

Graboids and Garland: The Ultimate Tremors-Themed Christmas Guide

12 Nights of Holiday Magic

The Power of Pause: 60-Second Mindfulness Practices

The Quick Reset: How to Reclaim Your Life After Burnout

The Shadow Eater: A Tale of Despair and Survival

The Micro-Mastery Method: Transform Your Skills in Just Minutes a Day

Reclaiming Time: How to Live More by Doing Less
Chronovore: The Eternal Nexus
The Mind Reset: Unlocking Your Inner Peace in a Chaotic World
Confidence Code: Building Unshakable Self-Belief
Baby the Vampire Terrier
Baby the Vampire Terrier's Christmas Adventure
Celestial Streams: The Content Creator's Astrology Manual
The Wealth Whisperer: Unlocking Abundance with Everyday Actions
The Energy Equation: Maximize Your Output Without Burning Out
The Happiness Algorithm: Science-Backed Steps to Joyful Living
Stress-Free Success: Achieving Goals Without Anxiety
Mindful Wealth: The New Blueprint for Financial Freedom
The Festive Flavors of New Year: A Culinary Celebration
The Master's Gambit: Keys of Eternal Power
Shadowed Secrets: Groundhog Day Mysteries
Beneath the Burrow: Lessons from the Groundhog
Spring's Whispers: The Groundhog's Prediction
The Limitless Mindset: Unlock Your Untapped Potential
The Focus Funnel: How to Cut Through Chaos and Get Results
Bold Moves: Building Courage to Live on Your Terms
The Daily Shift: Simple Practices for Lasting Transformation
The Quarter-Life Reset: Thriving in Your 20s and 30s
The Art of Shadowplay: Building Your Own Personal Myth
The Eternal Loop: Finding Purpose in Repetition
Burrowing Wisdom: Life Lessons from the Groundhog
Shadow Work: A Groundhog Day Perspective
Love in Bloom: 5-Minute Romantic Gestures
The Shadowspell Codex: Secrets of Forbidden Magick
The Burnout Cure: Finding Balance in a Busy World
The Groundhog Prophecy: Unlocking Seasonal Secrets
Nog Tales: The Spirited History of Eggnog

Six More Weeks: Embracing Seasonal Transitions

The Lumivian Chronicles: Fragments of the Fifth Dimension

Money on Your Mind: A Beginner's Guide to Wealth

The Focus Fix: Breaking Through Distraction

January's Spirit Keepers: Mystical Protectors of the Cold

Creativity Unchained: Unlocking Your Wildest Ideas in 2025

Manifestation Mastery: 365 Days to Rewrite Your Reality

The Groundhog's Mirror: Reflecting on Change

The Weeping Angels' Christmas Curse

Burrowed in Time: A Groundhog Day Journey

Heartbeats: Poems to Share with Your Valentine

Dino Wicca: The Sacred Grimoire of Prehistoric Magick

Courage of the Pride: Finding Your Inner Roar

The Lion's Leap: Bold Moves for Big Results

Healthy Hustle: Achieving Without Overworking

Practical Manifesting: Turning Dreams into Reality in 2025

Jurassic Pharaohs: Unlocking the Magick of Ancient Egypt and Dino Wicca

The Happiness Equation: Small Changes for Big Joy

The Confidence Compass: Finding Your Inner Strength

Whispers in the Hollow: Tales of the Forgotten Beasts

Echoes from the Hollow: The Return of Forgotten Beasts

The Hollow Ascendant: The Rise of the Forgotten Beasts

The Relationship Reset: Building Better Connections

Mastering the Morning: How to Win the Day Before 8 AM

The Shadow's Dance: Groundhog Day Symbolism

Cupid's Kitchen: Quick Valentine's Day Recipes

Valentine's Day on a Budget: Love Without Breaking the Bank

Astrocraft: Aligning the Stars in the World of Minecraft

Forecasting Life: Groundhog Day Reflections

Bleeding Hearts: Twisted Tales of Valentine's Terror

Herbal Smoke Revolution: The Ultimate Guide to Nature's Cigarette Alternative

Winter's Wrath: The Complete Survival Blueprint for Extreme Freezes.

The Groundhog's Shadow: A Tale of Seasons

Burrowed Insights: Wisdom from the Groundhog

Sensual Strings: The Art of Erotic Bondage

Whispered Flames: Unlocking the Power of Fire Play

Forgotten Shadows: A Guide to Cryptids Lost to Time

Six Weeks of Secrets: Groundhog Day's Hidden Messages

Shadows and Cycles: Groundhog Day Reflections

The Art of Love Letters: Crafting the Perfect Message

Romantic Getaways at Home: Turning Your Space into Paradise

Purrfect Brews: A Cat Lover's Guide to Coffee and Companionship

The Groundhog's Wisdom: Timeless Lessons for Modern Life

The Shadow Oracle: Groundhog Day as a Predictor

Emerging from the Burrow: A Journey of Renewal

The Language of Love: Learning Your Partner's Love Style

Authorpreneur: The Ultimate Blueprint for Writing, Publishing, and Thriving as an Author

Weathering the Seasons: Groundhog Day Perspectives

Valentine's Day Magic: A Guide to Romantic Rituals

The Shadow Chronicles: Stories of Groundhog Day

Love and Laughter: Fun Games for Valentine's Day

AstroRealty: Unlocking the Stars for Property Success

The Groundhog's Path: A Guide to Seasonal Balance

Groundhog Day Diaries: Reflections in the Shadow

The Groundhog's Light: Illuminating the Path Ahead

Valentine's Traditions from Around the World

AI Wealth Revolution: Unlocking the Trillionaire Mindset

Love Rekindled: Reigniting Passion in Relationships

Single and Thriving: Self-Love on Valentine's Day

Emerald Legends: Mystical Tales of Ireland

Green Alchemy: Harnessing Nature's Magic
The Hearts of Horror: A Valentine's Day Nightmare
The Leprechaun's Guide to Wealth and Wisdom
Dancing with the Sidhe: Celebrating the Otherworld
Shamrocks and Shadows: Mysteries of the Green Isle
Emerald Energy: Harnessing Luck and Growth
The Gingerbread Golem's Valentine: A Sweetheart's Guide to Love and Enchantment
The Celtic Knot: Weaving Life and Destiny
Green Fire: Elemental Magic for St. Patrick's Day
Clover Chronicles: Finding Your Inner Luck
Ireland's Mystical Creatures: A Field Guide
Gingerbread Golem's Love Almanac
Prowl and Thrive: The Lion's Guide to Success
Love Alchemy: Transforming Your Life Through Heart Energy
WORLD DOMINATION: Woman's Rule 3:The New Life
The Midnight Rose: A Guide to Lunar Love Spells
The Forbidden Letters: Writing Your Own Love Prophecy
Luck and Lore: St. Patrick's Day for Modern Mystics
The Green Path: A Pagan Celebration of Renewal
The Dark Architect's Guide to Reprogramming Reality
Prankster's Paradise: A Guide to Harmless Hijinks
Manifest Your Reality: The Law of Attraction Simplified
The TARDIS Owner's Manual: Understanding the Doctor's Ship: *A complete guide to the TARDIS, its technology, secrets, and mysteries*
Starlit Romance: Astrology Secrets for Finding True Love
The Time Lord's Atlas: A Complete Guide to the Whoniverse: ***A breakdown of the locations, planets, and dimensions explored in Doctor Who***
Sweetheart Shadows: The Dark Side of Love and Attraction
February Fire: Reigniting Passion in Every Area of Life

The Self-Love Toolkit: 5 Ways to Embrace Who You Are
February Sparks: Ignite Your Dreams in 28 Days
March to Success: A 31-Day Action Blueprint
Ancient Paths: The 13 Sacred Principles of Dino Wicca
Echoes of Tomorrow: Navigating the AI Revolution
The Wellness Blueprint: Balancing Mind, Body, and Soul
Green Horizons: Sustainable Living for a Better Tomorrow
The AI Wealth Code: How to Make Millions with Automation
AI-Powered Creativity: Writing, Art, and Music for Profit
Extinction Rites: Rebirthing Your Soul Through Prehistoric Magick
Sacred Serpents tarot
Celestial Enchantment blank journal
Star Strains
Culinary Journeys: Exploring Global Flavors at Home
The Hollowvale Curse
The Hollowvale Harvest
The Egg of Transformation: Awakening Your Inner Power
Blooming Into Power: A Wiccan Guide to Spring Awakening
The Nightmare Nexus: The Third Doctor's Perilous Haunting
Digital Detox: Reclaiming Your Life in a Connected World
Ostara's Path: Walking the Spiral of Renewal
The Sacred Hare
Financial Freedom: Building Wealth in the Modern Age
Spring's Cauldron: Stirring the Waters of Change
The Hollowvale Pact
Quantum Consciousness: The Science of Reality Shifting
The Hollowvale Hunger
The Sacred Waters Within: A Witch's Guide to Hydrocephalus Magick
The Raven's Nest: Building a Life of Unshakable Stability
AI and the Human Mind: The Future of Intelligence
The Hollowvale Reckoning

Timeless Love: Building and Maintaining Lasting Relationships

The Raven's Roar: Unlocking Unstoppable Confidence

Raven Sight: Awakening Intuition and Inner Wisdom

The Butterfly Effect: Small Changes, Big Transformations

Taming the Boogeyman: How to Conquer Your Inner Fears

The Magick of Green: Awakening Earth's Energy in You

The Entrepreneurial Mindset: Secrets to Business Success

The Hollowvale End

The Shadow Luck Ritual: Reclaiming Power from Your Dark Side

Spring Magick for Beginners: A Simple Guide to Seasonal Energy Work

Doctor Who: The Hollowvale Conundrum

The March of Miracles: Unlocking Synchronicities in Spring

Unveiling the Cosmos: A Guide to Stargazing and Space Exploration

The Ultimate Guide to Surviving an Economic Collapse

The AI Gold Rush: How to Profit from the AI Revolution

Bastet's Shadow: The Hidden Power of Feline Magick

The Bastet Codex: Unlocking the Goddess's Magickal Secrets

Purring Spells: Harnessing Bastet's Healing Frequencies

Bastet's Nine Lives: Rebirth, Transformation, and Immortality Spells

Primal Currents: Hydrocephalus Magick in the Path of Dino Wicca

The Digital Gold Rush: Mastering E-Commerce and Online Sales

Future Shock: Adapting to the Next Decade of Change

The Quantum Mindset: Think Like a Billionaire

Sacred Motherhood: Awakening the Divine Feminine Within

The Mother's Spellbook: Enchantments for Love, Protection, and Prosperity

The Witch's Guide to Parenting: Raising Empowered and Intuitive Children

The Magick of Motherhood: Reclaiming Your Power Through Rituals

The Pagan Path to Self-Love: A Goddess's Guide to Worth and Confidence

Wild Woman Magick: Unleashing Your Primal Power

The Money Magnet Blueprint: Unlocking Unlimited Wealth

Biohacking 101: Unlock Your Body's Full Potential

The Wild Father: A Pagan Guide to Strength and Wisdom

The Sacred Masculine: Unlocking Your Inner Power

The Druid's Compass

The Warrior's Mindset

The Father's Fire

Odin's Path

Ancestral Bonds

The House That Whispers

The Magician's Code

The Wild Hunt

The Green Man's Path

The Altar of Success

The Shadow and the Sword

The High Priestess's Guide to Energy Healing

The Lunar Mother

The Sacred Self-Care Grimoire

The Womb Wisdom Codex

The Wheel of the Mother

The Witch's Guide to Manifestation

The Q2 Reset

The Ultimate Guide to AI-Powered Passive Income

Escape the 9-5

AI Feline Fortunes

The Tear-Stained Grimoire

Razorblade Runes
Cemetery Sirens
The Midnight Wristwatch
The Town That Forgets
AI Horror & Creepypasta
The Hollow Frequency
The Breach Echo
The Quiet Between Worlds
The Sigil of Tharan-Khul
Summon the Vault of Y'ha'ten
The Becoming Codex
The Profit of Az'ra-nar
The Drowned Logos
Echoes of the Eldritch Will
The Deep Ledger
Necronomicon of Networth
Covenant of the Wealthwyrm
The Whisperer's Manifesto
The Rites of Azh-K'luth
The Ark of the Crawling Coin
The Tithe of Shadows
Inkheart Abyss
The Timewinds of Y'ha-nthlei
The Spiral Labyrinth of Azag-Nirrh
The Gallifreyan Heresy of the Black Pharaoh
The Psalms of Nyog-Sotha
Black Rain Alchemy
The Infinite Maw
The Entropic Blueprint
The Oracle of Sh'guul
The Book of Breach
The Drowned Saint's Testament
Dreamcraft of the Sleeper God

The Silence Market
Cthonomics: The Dark Wealth Algorithm
Invocation of the Ten-Eyed King
Wealthbound to the Wyrm Below
Become the Unnameable
Codex of the Sovereign Flame
Rituals of Relentless Becoming
The Shadow Ascends
The Eyes Beneath You
The Will That Wakes Worlds
Silence Is a Weapon
The Mirror That Screams
The Whisper Between Moments
The Mind That Devours Fear
The Myth of the Finished Self
The Architect of Your Madness
The Voice You've Buried
The Discipline of Madness
Stormborn: Awakening Your Inner Tempest
The Mind That Ate Time
Unbind Your Becoming
The Pact You Owe Yourself
The Devourer's Diet
The Acid That Carves the Path
The Tower You Must Burn
The Breath Between Worlds
Speak Like the Deep
The Labyrinth Within
The Spine of the Sea God
Rejection Is a Portal
The Crown You Refused
The Scar Is the Spell
The Lightless Flame

The Habit of Becoming Horrific
ChickenJockey Chaos
The Gatekeeper Within
You Are Not Your Name
The Compass of the Mad
The Archive of Unsent Letters
What the Mirror Can't Show You
The Knife You Needed
Worship Nothing, Become Everything
The Other Voice
The Body the World Forgot
The Vein of the Void
The Black Bone Codex
The Puzzle of the Hidden Self (Millennium Puzzle)
The Eye That Sees the Lie *(Millennium Eye)*
The Ring of Return (Millennium Ring)
The Rod of Relentless Will ***(Millennium Rod)***
The Tally of the Soul (Millennium Tauk/Necklace)
The Key to the Locked Timeline (Millennium Key)
The Scale of Sacred Decisions (Millennium Scales)
Inferno Bites: The UnOfficial Minecraft Lava Cookbook
Rot in the Attic
Prana: The Hidden Force of Your Infinite Self
The Shadow Realm Within: Transforming Darkness Into Destiny
The Borderland Collapse
Claws of Protection: Bastet's Defensive Magick
Mr. Ring-a-Ding's Madness
Yugioh Astrology: Celestial Deckcraft and Duel Destiny (2026–2027 Edition)
The Seal You Signed: Unlocking the Power You Once Feared
The Puzzle of Infinite Minds: Unlocking the Mentalism Hidden Within

The Eye That Mirrors the All: Secrets of Inner Reflection
Doctor Who: The Toymaker's Broadcast
The Rod of Eternal Flow: Commanding the Currents of Vibration
Golden Eyes of Bastet: Enhancing Psychic Vision
The Key of Dual Forces: Balance Within the Polarity
The Scales of Living Rhythm: Timing the Dance of Life
The Necklace of Hidden Cause: Weaving the Webs of Fate
The Ring of Secret Masters: Rising Through the All Within All
Daggers of the Dying Deep
Bastet's Wealth and Fortune Magick: Prosperity Rituals of the Goddess
The Tide that Speaks
The Scrolls of Petosiris: 13 Rituals from the Feathered Eye
Petosiris and the Living Plague of Osirion
Feline Fire: Bastet's Passion and Love Magick
The Star Altar of Petosiris
Bastet's Whiskers: Supernatural Sensory Magick
The Bastet Grimoire
Feeding the Shadows
The Mouthless Prayer
The Spiral Wound
Becoming the Ibis: Lessons from Petosiris's Mind
The Crimson Coven: Cola Magick for Sweet Dominion
Sacred Cat's Paw
The Soda Zodiac: A Flavor for Every Sign
Covenant of the Crawling Flame
The Ink of Ish'Zur
Frothroot: The Thirst That Ate the World
The Golden Glyphs of Prosperity
The Etherbind Codex
Echoes of the Resistance: Reclaiming the You That Survived

Harnessed Minds: Breaking Free from Mental Control
The Eyes in the Smoke
Rootwake: The Carbon Covenant
Skitter Logic: Unlearning the Fear That Built You
Doctor Who: The World That Froths
Rootwake: The Fizz That Rewrites Flesh
Rootwake: Frothfather of the World
The Holly Pact: Blood Beneath the Mistletoe
The 2nd Mass Principle: Building Unbreakable Tribes
Web of Wits: A Survival Guide to Encounters with Anasi the Spider (Aunt Nancy)
The Hexbreaking Handbook: Effective Spells to Remove Curses
Pop Alchemy: Transform Your Life One Sip at a Time
The Mason Code: Leading in Unleadable Times
Petosiris and the Fifth Chamber of Thoth
The Ether Seed Within
The Parent of Tomorrow
Petosiris's Pyramid of Perpetual Wealth
Unlearn the World
Grimoire of the Hollow Tongue
Zodiac Weeds: Finding Your Strain Through the Stars
Aquarius Rises in the Bank
The Sugar God's Smile
The Skinclock Reversal: Biohacking the Face of Time
Debtburn: How to Obliterate What You Owe Forever
The Ice Cream Oracle: What Your Cone Says About Your Future
Silence Is Sovereignty: The Power of Being Unreadable
The Wind That Whispers Through Stone
Path of the Four Directions
Doctor Who: The Maestro's Symphony of Endings
Oxygen Grail: Breathing to Undo the Clock

Zodiacal Collapse: When Stars Devour Time
Teachings from the Red Sand Silence
Doctor Who: Omega – The Broken Equation
Memory Wipe Your Past: Start Over Like a MiB
Mitochondria Prime: Ignite the Core of Youth
A Nest of Roaches
Grub from the Galaxy: MiB Recipes You'll Never Forget
Whiskers of Power: Bastet's Guide to Inner Sovereignty
The Gift Must Cost Them: Negotiation Through Unequal Exchange
The Worm Guys' Wealth Code: Hustle Like an Alien
Bug Out: The Edgar Method for Ruthless Goal Setting
Weaving Life with Spiderwoman's Pattern
Doctor Who: The Rani's Renaissance
How to Get a Job (If You're a Puppygirl)
Speak Through Others: The Art of Proxy Power
T-Rex Your Trauma: Reclaim the Power of Your Primal Self
The Black Briefcase: How MiB Stay Wealthy in Silence
The Thirst Beyond Reason: Understanding Diabetes Insipidus From the Inside Out
Backwoods Witchcraft for Billionaires: The Pagan Path from Dirt Roads to Gold Roads
The Moonshine Grimoire: Fermented Spells for Abundance
The Nameless Geometry
The Wraith's Mixtape: Spellcasting with Songs of Sorrow
The Gallifreyan Gentleman: Silent Wealth, Sonic Confidence, and the Doctor's Code of Living
Sugar Water Confidence
Dino Totems: Spirit Guides from Earth's First Gods
Pumpkin Sigils & Ritual Smoke
The Hózhó Compass
The Distortus Discipline – Order from Inner Mutation
Witchcraft for the Cold-Blooded Soul

Moonlight Over the Blessingway
Water, Interrupted: When the Body Forgets How to Hold On
Deformed but Divine: Embracing Your Asymmetry
Hexes in the Henhouse: The Farm Witch's Guide to Power
The Reversed Flame: A Grimoire of Inverted Power
Salt, Cells, and Sanity: Reclaiming Balance with Diabetes Insipidus
King of the Broken: Crowning the Flawed Self
Moonlight Scars: Emo Moon Magick and the Art of Lunar Sorrow
Noose Spells: Magick of the Hanging Rope
The Goth Cathedral: Rituals of the Broken and Beautiful
The Cretaceous Codex: Dino Spirits and Fossil Magick
The Turkey Bones Ritual
Nine Lives of Manifestation: Unlocking Bastet's Reality Codes
Chaos Muscles: Building Strength from Twisted Pain
Emo Blood Magick: The Veins of Power
The 3AM Flood: Nighttime Urination, Sleep Loss, and the DI Spiral
The Silence Between the Stars
The Lemon Method: Sour Your Way to Success
Starlit Sovereign
The Rite of Twelve Gates: Walking the Gates of the Duat.
Cornbread and Conjure: Recipes for Riches and Rootwork
The Black Rose Rituals: Emo Love Spells and Obsession Magick
The Eternal Goodbye: Death Magick and Rebirth Rituals
Sinkrot: The Drain That Remembers
The Hybrid Mindset: Thinking Beyond Evolution
Bone Dry: Navigating Dehydration Before It Breaks You
Wreathcraft: Winter Sigils and Yuletide Spells
The Rite of Twelve Mouths

S'mores of the Damned: Haunted Recipes for Halloween Night

Rethink the Drink: A Beverage Survival Guide for DI Warriors

The Shadow Chord: Guitar Magick and Sonic

Malformed Yet Majestic: Leading When You Feel Wrong Inside

The Cursed Diary: Ink-Stained Spells of the Emo Soul

Anxiety Off Switch: Emergency Reset for a Fried Nervous System

The Energy Heist: How to Take Back Your Life from Drainers

Beyond the Bathroom: Rebuilding Your Social Life With DI

Coyote's Gift for Decision Makers

Ghoul-Goo: Spooky S'mores You'll Die For

Echoes in the Mirror: Scrying and Self-Destruction Magick

Thread and Thorn: Stitching Spells from Rural Cloth

The Mogwai Mind: Building Untouchable Wealth from Small Ideas

Be Your Own Guide: Trust Your Inner Compass

Hormones in Chaos: The Endocrine Puzzle of Diabetes Insipidus

ChronoCleanse: Detox Your Biological Timeline

The Limb You Hide Is the One That Saves You

Leaves, Bones, and Whisper Spells

The Dinosaur Mindset: Prehistoric Tactics for Modern Wealth

Clawing Back Control: A Bastet Method for Boundaries and Empowerment

Samhain Codes of the Forgotten

Orange Alchemy: The Autumnal Spellbook

Monster Within, Master Without

The Sigil That Sleeps

Hearthcraft: Yule Hearth Sigils and Winter Warmth Spells

Temple of the Purring Moon: Rituals from Bastet's Lineage
When the Earth Remembers Your Footsteps
Food for Mood: Eat to Heal Depression, Not Just Survive It
Witch of the Kudzu Vine: Southern Pagan Wealth Secrets
The Invisible Diagnosis: Advocating for Yourself With DI
The Coffin's Lullaby: Sleep Magick and Nightmares as Portals
Ashes of the Will: Rituals for Erasing the Self
The Fracture Rite: Shattering the Magickal Core
Funeral Candles: The Art of Emo Flame Magick
The Black Grimoire: A Blank Ritual for Writing in Absence
Phantom Thirst: A Halloween Survival Guide for Diabetes Insipidus
The Hollow Crown: Emo Royalty and Magick of the Outcast King
Sandpainting for the Soul
Falling Into Balance: Using the Extra Hour to Recalibrate Life
100 Southern Superstitions That Still Work
The DI Child: A Parent's Guide to Raising Hydrated, Happy Kids
The Jungle of Shame: Escaping the Hidden Lab of Doubt
The Witch's Toast: S'mores Spells and Creepy Confections
The Hoodoo Pantry: Spells from the Mason Jar
The Immortal Fortune: Secret Wealth Lessons from Captain Jack Harkness
The Specter's Embrace: Magick for Channeling Ghostly Lovers
Grateful Waters: A Thanksgiving Survival Guide for Diabetes Insipidus
The Seizure Gospel
Harvestbind: Autumn Sigils and Samhain Spells
Doctor Who: The Algorithmic Awakening
Silent Nights, Steady Waters: A Christmas Survival Guide for Diabetes Insipidus

The Extra Hour Effect: How One Hour Can Transform Everything

Blade Between the Breaths

Running with the Mountain Shadows

Echoes of the Failed Experiment – Becoming a Living Legacy

Swamp Witches & River Ghosts: Real Southern Hauntings

Cornbread Prophecies: Magical Recipes from a Southern Table

Doctor Who: The Signal in the Star

Bloomcraft: Spring Sigils and Equinox Enchantments

Vanisher: How to Disappear from the Internet Without Losing Your Life

The Ultimate Christmas Cookie Cookbook

The Unbreakable Parent: How to Mentally Survive Raising Kids in a Broken World

Time Debt: How to Reclaim the Hours You Didn't Know You Lost

One Month, One Million: Unconventional Cash Creation Tactics

Doctor Who: The Cyber Conversion Protocol

Black Friday Frenzy: The Art of Finding Hidden Online Deals

The Grimoire Buried Under the Apple Tree

Digital Couponing Masterclass: Your Step-by-Step Guide to Black Friday Savings

The Fire Inside the Flint

Shadows on the Ceiling: The Emo Guide to Astral Magick

The Bone-Eaters Beneath Us

Black Friday Bundle Blueprint: Creating Irresistible Product Packages for Maximum Sales

Thirteen Nights of Unbinding

Doctor Who: Engines of Influence

Pumpkin Spice Alchemy: Recipes of Fire and Frost

When Raptor Met Rexy: Prehistoric Lessons in Wild Romance
Oblivion's Candle: Burn the Path Behind You
Campfire Curses and Chocolate: A Halloween S'mores Grimoire
The Wallet That Wasn't Mine: Breaking Free from Inherited Scarcity
The Cola Zodiac: What Your Fizz Says About Your Fate
Frostfire Fortune: Unlocking Winter's Hidden Prosperity
Signal Jamming: Detox Your Brain from Info Overload
The Dust of the Forgotten Rite
The Golden Cat Sigils: Drawing Power in Bastet's Name
Mud Magick: The Prosperity of Getting Dirty
Savory Spicefall: Beyond the Pumpkin Pie
Pumpkin Spice Apothecary Kitchen
The Pumpkin Spice Economy: Turning Trends into Billions
The Ember Veil: 13 Nights of Fire Magick
Financial Freeze: When Earning Triggers Panic
The Gingerbread Alchemist: Sweet Recipes with a Twist
Biosynth Power: Programming Yourself from Scratch
Echoes from the Talking Circle
Truffle Alchemy: Fungus of Fortune
Spores of Power: The Truffle Witch's Handbook
Doctor Who: The Tower That Speaks
The Mycelium Veil: Truffle Magick Unbound
Broke But Ashamed: Healing the Shame Wound of Debt
The Evergreen Mind: Growth Through Winter Stillness
The Black Veil Truffle Rite
The Voice Beneath Symbols
Witchlight on the Bayou: Swamp Spells for Sovereignty
I Grew Up Poor and Now I Sabotage My Success
The Lantern of Hollow Souls

Shutdown Survival: A Citizen's Guide to Thriving When Government Stops

When Abundance Feels Like a Threat: Healing the Hidden Fears of Enough

The Scarecrow Grimoire

Owls of the October Veil

Candlewax and Curses: A Halloween Spellbook

Excavating the Inner Fossil – Transforming Fossilized Thoughtforms into Tools of Power

The Yule Witch's Spellbook: Magick for the Holiday Season

Haunted Christmas: Ghost Stories for Winter Nights

The Christmas Survival Guide: Thriving Through the Chaos

The Bone Orchard Rites

Haunted Commerce: The Ghost in the Marketplace

When Money Triggers the Inner Child

Silent Night with the Silence: A Christmas Thriller

The Lightning Crown: Living and Leading Through Seizures

TARDIS Tidings: Festive Stories from the Whoniverse

Autumn Reset: Slowing Down Without Falling Behind

The Trillion Dollar Soul: Rewriting the Currency of Reality

Truffle Eclipse Magick

Micro-Manifestations: Quick Magick That Works

5-Minute Rituals for Busy Witches

The Marshmallow Massacre: Halloween Treats with a Sinister Twist

Blood and Blackberry Thorns

Magickal Mornings: Rituals for a Blessed Christmas Day

Embers of the All-Hallows Fire

The Pumpkin Market Collapse

The Hour You Gained: Transforming Time Into Power

The Chamber Must Be Sealed: Mastering the Power of Controlled Access

The Cursed Manuscript of Petosiris

10 Secrets to Surviving Holiday Crowds
The Witch's Dow Jones
The Witches' Graveyard Shift
Pumpkin Sigils: Carving Rites for Midnight Power
The Secret Shopper's Black Friday Guide: How to Get Early Access and VIP Deals
Fever in the Foundation
The Neuralyzer Reset: Reprogram Your Morning Routine
Lightning Lessons of the White Painted Woman
The Enchanted Snowflake
The Magic Sip: Surviving Disney Parks with Diabetes Insipidus
The One Who Draws Through You
Santa's Secrets: A Magical Holiday Planner
Silent Bells, Loud Miracles: Self-Help for the Season of Stillness
The Sugar Spell Codex: Confectionary Magick of Christmas
Autumn Hexcraft: Fallen Leaves, Fallen Barriers
Sleep Like a Fortress: Build a Life Where Insomnia Can't Survive
Nowhere Was Ever Home
Christmas Under the Stars: A Celestial Holiday Guide
Rentproof: How to Never Be Evicted Again
Workless: Escape the 9-5 Without Being Broke
The Gilded Gift: A Wealth Altar for Christmas Morning
The Black Friday Grimoire
The Hollowing: Ceremonies of Spiritual Collapse
Doctor Who: The Nameless Signal
Where the Eagle Hides His Courage
The Dwarf Tyrant's Ascent: Claiming Power in a World of Giants
The Currency of the Dead: Trading with Spectral Bankers
The Icebound Witch: Survival and Magick in the Cold

The Emergency Money Mind: Constant Crisis, Zero Calm

Thirst & Roses: A Valentine's Survival Guide for Diabetes Insipidus

Springing Into Clarity: Mastering the Energy Shift of Daylight Saving

Speed of the Nanotyrant: Agile Strategies for Life's Hunt

The 90-Day Reset: A Science-Backed Guide to Reinvent Yourself Before the New Year

The Coil of Thorns

Timegates Unleashed

Dopamine Fasting 2.0: Rewiring Your Brain in a World of Overstimulation

The Nanotyrannus Mutation: Embracing Your Differentiated Form

Unwritten January: How to Use the Blank Page of the Year to Re-Author Your Life

Feast of the Forgotten Spirits: Ancestor Magick for the Holidays

The Burnout Codex: A System for Thriving Beyond Stress

I Don't Deserve to Have Money

When the King Doesn't See You: The Shadow Predator's Guide

The Reset Ritual :A Guide to Shedding Last Year's Weight—Emotional and Physical—by Spring Cleaning Your Soul

Calendar Alchemy: Learn to Bend Time and Productivity around Your Natural Rhythms

The Mirror Contract: A One-Sentence Agreement with Yourself that Unlocks Real Change

The Nile Formula: Sacred Flow for Millionaire Minds

Forward Momentum: Productivity Rituals for the Lost Hour

Harvest Gold: Wealth Magick of Pumpkin Spice Commerce

The Magick of Christmas Lights: Illuminating Holiday Rituals

Cranberry Crown: Royal Self-Worth through Ritual Meals

Petosiris and the Worms of the Feathered Throne

The Evergreen Equation: Self-Help for Sustained Growth

The Rain Will Wash Us Away: Emo Weather Magick

Snowlight Shadows: Magick Under Frozen Stars

Doctor Who: Merger of Empires

The Light Within the Feast: Magickal Wealth of Yuletide Flame

Momentum Machines: Small Habits Designed to Snowball into Unstoppable Forward Motion

Calm Spells: Magickal Solutions for Anxiety Relief

Santa's Final List: The Naughty Never Leave

The Mystic's Guide to Banishing Worry

The Silence Dividend: Turning Quiet Mornings into Compounding Growth All Year

Charmed Stillness: Rituals to Ease the Mind

Blood Spiral Ascension

The Vanishing Heart Invocation

Crystal Calm: Harnessing Stones for Anxiety

The Nano Tyrant Code: Strength in the Small Predator

The Energy Ledger: Accounting Methods for Vitality, Not Just Money

Snowglobe Mindset: Shake Up Your Thoughts, Settle Into Peace

The Weight of the Feather: Anubis's Codes for Soul Balance

Pocket Peppermint Power: Tiny Rituals for Big Holiday Energy

Shadowkeeper of the Golden Jackal: Anubis's Path to Energetic Protection

The Witch's Breath: Anxiety Relief Through Magickal Breathing

The Tiny Ember: Pocket Motivation for Cold Days

Stocking Sorcery: Mini Spells for Holiday Luck and Prosperity

Warm Hands, Steady Heart: Micro Grounding for Winter Anxiety

The Jackal's Lantern: Guide-Lights for Walking the Dark Path

Anubis's Silent Steps: Rituals for Stealth, Peace & Emotional Quiet

The Bonewake Protocol

Extinction-Proof: How to Outlive Trends, Trauma, and Time

The Fourth Doctor: The Eccentric Wanderer

The Second Doctor: Chaos and Charm in the TARDIS (Patrick Troughton, 1966–1969)

The Third Doctor: Earthbound Defender of Time (Jon Pertwee, 1970–1974)

The First Doctor: Genesis of the Time Lord (William Hartnell, 1963–1966)

The Fourth Doctor: The Eccentric Wanderer ***(Tom Baker, 1974–1981)***

The Fifth Doctor: Elegance and Empathy (Peter Davison, 1982–1984)

The Sixth Doctor: A Kaleidoscope of Conflict (Colin Baker, 1984–1986)

The Seventh Doctor: The Strategist of Shadows (Sylvester McCoy, 1987–1989)

The Eighth Doctor: A Time Lord's Renaissance (Paul McGann, 1996)

The War Doctor: A Time Lord's Burden (John Hurt, 2013)

The Ninth Doctor: The Healer of Worlds

(Christopher Eccleston, 2005)

The Tenth Doctor: The Lonely Hero (David Tennant, 2005–2010)

The Eleventh Doctor: The Madman in a Box (Matt Smith, 2010–2013)

The Twelfth Doctor: The Rebel with a Cause (Peter Capaldi, 2013–2017)

The Thirteenth Doctor: Breaking the Mold
(Jodie Whittaker, 2017–2022)

The Fourteenth Doctor: A New Beginning (David Tennant, 2022–2023)

The Fifteenth Doctor: Rewriting the Stars
(Ncuti Gatwa, 2023–2025)

Santa's Shortcut to Success: Micro Habits for a Better New Year

The Midnight Cocoa Manifesto: Comfort Rituals for Hard Nights

Why I Can't Save: Trauma Blocks to Financial Planning

Dino Brain, Mega Goals: Rewire Yourself for Savage Success.

Jurassic Profit: Unearth Your Inner Millionaire Fossil

Scales & Softness: Dating with Dino Heart

Carnotaurus Dreams.

Red Willow Thinking.

Reindeer Resilience: How to Keep Going When You're Exhausted

Candlewick Courage: Lighting Strength in Dark Seasons.

Elf-Mode Focus: Fast Attention Fixes for Busy Seasons

Futureproof Feelings: Emotional Skill-Building for Resilience No Matter What the New Year Brings

The 90-Day Rewire: Transform Your Neural Pathways Before Spring Blooms

Jolly Rich: Christmas Micro-Money Magick for Fast Prosperity.

Gingerbread Gratitude: Mini Practices for a Happier Holiday

Trauma-Spending: When Money Becomes a Drug

Goal Skeletons: Build Minimalist Frameworks for Resolutions That Last

The Snarl Strategy: Growling Back at a World That Silenced You

The Hourglass Reset: Reclaiming What the Clock Took

Yule Claw: Dino Rites of Light in the Darkness

Sacred Circles: Grounding Rituals for Anxious Souls

Clockstopper's Gut: Rebuilding the Core of Time

Winterfire Drive: Harness the Cold Season's Stillness to Ignite Deep Motivation

The 5-Minute Productivity Hack: Small Steps to Big Results

Light Ascending: A Self-Help Guide to Longer Days

Inner Economy: Trade Self-Doubt for Confidence Like a High-Value Currency

Simple Success: Decluttering Your Life for Better Results

The Resilient Mind: Thriving in Tough Times

The 2026 Playbook: Mastering the Year Ahead

The Spring Sleep Solution: Conquering Fatigue After Time Change.

The Hormonal Compass: Navigate Back to Your Youth

Golden Vision: Eating for Your Eye Color with the Power of Ghee

Lionhearted Love: Strength in Relationships

MiB Mindset: Think Like a Cosmic Agent

The Ladder of Small Wins: Climb Out of Stagnation by Stacking Micro-Victories

The Momentum Hour: Gaining More in Less Time.

The Year of You: A Self-Help Blueprint for Unapologetic Self-Ownership

The Dust That Watches You Back.

The Astral Parent

Shadow of the King: The Nanotyrannus Parable

Tiny Tidings of Triumph: Small Wins That Change Your Life

Dwarf Tyrant Rising: When You're the One They Overlook

The Bank Account Mirror: Healing How You See Yourself Through Money

Cretaceous Black

When Love Costs Too Much: Romantic Triggers and Financial Wounds

Dream-Eater's Guide to Wealth

Unzipped Reality: The Jacket That Opens Portals

The Power of No: How to Set Boundaries and Get Rich

Keeper of the Desert Veil: Anubis's Teachings on Illusion & Truth

Redacted Stargates: Stories the SGC Buried

The Clock That Dripped Time

Doctor Who: The Silent Acquisition

Hairline Manifestation: Unlocking Power at the Edge of Thought

Cash-Eater Crickets: How Insects Predict Economic Collapse

Dead Pet Whisperer: Grief Alchemy from the Other Side

The Love Algorithm Is Broken: Hack Romance Before It Hacks You

The Rite of the 8-Limbed Seal

Melt the Moon: A Fire Ritual to Reshape Emotion

Venomous Miracles: Healing Through the Poison Path

Wealth Without Water: The Post-Aquatic Rich Life

The Butterfly Betrayal: When Change Turns on You

The Quiet Upgrade: How Humans Are Secretly Rebuilding Themselves Without Asking Permission

Nobody Taught Us This: The Missing Human Manual for Money, Energy, and Self-Respect

You Were Never Broken: Why Most People Are Reacting Normally to an Unstable World

After the Noise Ends: How Humans Reset When the World Finally Goes Quiet

The Month That Tells the Truth: Why January Reveals What the Rest of the Year Hides

Tremors Party Unleashed: The Ultimate Guide to a Graboids Birthday Bash

Cold Start Human: Rebooting Motivation Without Forcing Momentum

The Year that doesn't start until they say

Love Without Performance: What Connection Looks Like When No One Is Watching

February Is a Mirror: What Love Exposes About You

How We Learned Love Wrong: Uninstalling Cultural Myths About Connection

You Are Not Too Much: Why Needing Love Is Not a Flaw

The Crooked Fence Covenant: Backwoods Boundaries and Witch Wealth

The Day That Keeps Repeating: Why Your Life Feels Stuck—and How to Shift It Gently

Nothing Changes Until Something Softens: Escaping Repetition Without Violence to Yourself

Same Life, Different Ending: How Tiny Choices Rewrite Repetition

The Loop Isn't Punishment: Why You're Being Asked to Learn, Not Suffer

Panic at the Register: Retail Anxiety and Public Shame

The Secret Formula to Becoming an Influencer in 90 Days

The New Rich: How to Retire by 35

Digital Nomad Secrets: How to Travel the World and Make Millions

Burn Your Waiting Room: Escape the Delay Spiral

Strapped for Pleasure: A Complete Guide to Pegging and Strap-On Play

Locked in Desire: A Guide to Chastity Play and Intimate Control

Burrowing into History: Groundhog Day Through the Ages
The Shadow Forecast: The Science of Groundhog Day
Choice Cascades: How One Decision in January Sets Ripples for the Whole Year
The Anti-Anxiety Blueprint: Mastering Fear and Stress for Success
The Ancestral Path of the Jackal Priest
Winterborn Titans: Giants of Ice and Stone
The Extinction Spire
The Emotion That Made Me Millions
Delete Their Voice: Become Unreachable
The Frostbound Mysteries: Mythical Beings of January's Chill
The Roar Within: Unlocking Your Potential
From Burrow to Sky: Groundhog Day Explained
The Boogey Book: Festive Ward-Off Edition
Fooled Ya! The Psychology Behind Great Pranks
April Fools' Alchemy: Transforming Everyday Items into Pranks
Anchor Habits: Root Yourself in Unshakable Routines That Endure Seasonal Change
Emerald Waters: A St. Patrick's Day Survival Guide for Diabetes Insipidus
The Groundhog's Legacy: Myths, Legends, and Facts
Six Weeks of Mystery: The Truth Behind Groundhog Day
The Upgrade Mind: Tech-Like Patches and Updates for Your Mental Operating System
Moon Blood, Star Flesh: Embracing Your Hybrid Nature
Groundhog Lore and Legend: A Complete Guide
You Are the Lie They Can't Kill
Download a Different Reality
The Quiet Advantage: Winning Without Announcing Yourself
A Year of Gratitude: Unlocking Joy

Get Some Tarot cards: https://www.makeplayingcards.com/sell/apophis-occult-shop

Get some shirts: https://www.bonfire.com/store/apophis-shirt-emporium/

<u>Instagrams:</u>
@apophis_enterprises,
@apophisbookemporium,
@apophisscardshop
Twitter: @apophisenterpr1
Tiktok:@apophisenterprise
Youtube: @sg1fan23477
Hive: @sg1fan23477
CheeLee: @SG1fan23477

Podcast: Apophis Chat Zone: https://open.spotify.com/show/5zXbrCLEV2xzCp8ybrfHsk?si=fb4d4fdbdce44dec

Newsletter: https://apophiss-newsletter-27c897.beehiiv.com/

If you want to support me or see posts of other projects that I have come over to: **buymeacoffee.com/mpetchinskg**

I post there daily several times a day

www.ingramcontent.com/pod-product-compliance
Lightning Source LLC
LaVergne TN
LVHW022232200926
848481LV00006B/2231